It's Over!

How to End a Relationship and Feel Good About Yourself

Elsabe Smit

Copyright

ISBN-13: 978-1516976201
ISBN-10:1516976207

Table of Contents

Chapter 1: Why Do We Have Relationships?   1

Chapter 2: The Mechanics of a Relationship   14

Chapter 3: Your Emotional Cycles   28

Chapter 4: What is True Love?   50

Chapter 5: How to End a Relationship   57

Chapter 6: What is Keeping You in the Relationship? 66

Chapter 7: The Future of Relationships   96

About The Author   101

More from This Author   104

When you see this symbol throughout the book, pause and reflect. Make notes, answer the question or complete the exercise.

Chapter 1: Why Do We Have Relationships?

In this chapter you will learn

- Why we have relationships

- What a soul contract is and why it is formed.

- The importance of looking beyond the surface for the other side of the truth.

- The importance of self-love.

This book is about ending relationships successfully. We all have to end a relationship at some point in our lives, whether it is a romantic, friendly, work or other relationship.

The book will focus on love relationships, because that is always closest to our hearts and cause the most pain. However, the processes and rules that are discussed in this book apply to all relationships.

How do you end a relationship successfully?

You remove the emotional pain that often goes with ending a relationship.

Yes, it is that simple, but it also requires a lot of focused work.

We all have our story to tell. This story is made up entirely of past history that we re-live based on our own perspective. This past history prevents us from getting a balanced view and accepting ourselves. Our interpretation of events also creates many alibis – good reasons why things 'go wrong' and why we are 'not in control'.

Once we understand why a relationship was formed in the first place, it becomes so much easier to end the relationship with Love and gratitude. We remove the self-imposed obstacles and get much closer to the life we want for ourselves.

This does not mean that ending a troubled relationship is always the correct thing to do. The book will help you understand whether your relationship is going through an interesting, challenging period, or coming to a natural end.

 Do you believe in your heart of hearts that there is still a future for the relationship that you are concerned about?

There are times when you will apply the knowledge gained from this book so that a relationship can move forward and grow stronger. There are other times when the relationship comes to an end, and your knowledge will help you navigate that end with ease and gratitude.

Either way, **as long as a relationship causes you emotional pain, it holds you back and you need to take some action to remove the pain and the obstacle.** If you wait for someone else to take such action, let me assure you it will not happen. Taking action to resolve any relationship you are in is your task and yours alone. There is no shared guilt or shared burden when you are desperately unhappy.

Yes, it is true that there are at least two people in a relationship. That does not mean you share the responsibility for dealing with the relationship or resolving it.

Understanding why you are in a relationship is part of your own journey through life, regardless of what your partner in the relationship does. Your task is to take 100% responsibility for your relationship, and to complete your own inner process when you experience a crisis in this relationship.

What would you say is wrong with your relationship? If you have already left the relationship, what would you say went wrong and made you leave?

Draw four columns on a sheet of paper.

Add these four headings to the columns:

- **What my partner did wrong**
- **What other people did wrong**
- **Where the circumstances went wrong**
- **What I did wrong.**

List as many causes for the break-up of the relationship in these columns as you want to. If you need to make a longer list, continue on a separate sheet. Don't worry about how long your list is or where exactly the blame should lie. The purpose of this exercise is just to get your thoughts on paper. You will get back to this exercise later on.

Why Is a Relationship Formed?

This book is not about religion, although some concepts that relate to religion will apply here.

If you have strong religious beliefs, this book will make you re-evaluate those beliefs and probably take you to a better understanding of your beliefs.

If you have no religious beliefs, this book will add to your self-knowledge.

The book deals with universal truths – in other words truths that are present in most religions as well as outside of any religion.

If you believe in eternal life, then this is your opportunity to gain clarity about it.

If you do not believe in eternal life, let's assume for the purposes of the discussion that eternal life does exist. Once you have completed the book, you can always change your mind if you want to.

Lots of research has been done on past life regression. This research can probably be interpreted as flawed because it has a very individual slant.

However, the research that always has consistent findings across cultures and age groups relate to what happens during the break between lives, rather than during a previous or future life.

Imagine eternal life as a never-ending piece of string. Any one life that we live forms a tiny part of that piece of string.

We are born onto this earth with a life script based on our progress in our eternal life.

Before we come into this life, we enter into a soul contract with all the people we share our lives with. These soul contracts are agreed before we are born.

In some instances, we are with people right from the moment of birth, for example our parents and siblings.

We meet our other contractual partners throughout our lives.

We forget the reason for our relationships and the contracts as soon as we enter this world. This is because our focus initially turns to the basics of survival, and later to growing up.

During our lives we meet people and there is an instant attraction – or an instant repulsion. This attraction or repulsion is experienced as a physical response that we like to refer to as 'chemistry'.

For the moment we will focus on the attraction rather than the repulsion – because we will not enter into love relationships where there is an instant repulsion.

This instant attraction or 'chemistry' is in fact a spiritual response to the other person – where both parties experience the same 'sense of knowing' about their soul contract.

This attraction is followed by a period of infatuation – where the other person can do nothing wrong. If they do things that we dislike, we turn a blind eye and justify their actions to suit our perceptions. For example, if a man drinks a little bit too much for her liking, the woman might say to herself 'All I need to do is love him more, and he will not need to drink'. Or where a woman is not too concerned about the state of her house, a man will say 'Well, she is a lovely person and can hold a good conversation'. This is part of the soul contract, as you will see later on.

Have you experienced this 'chemistry' or immediate connection with anyone? Think back to the situation. How did you know that the romantic relationship or friendship was 'right' for you?

What Is The Purpose Of The Soul Contract?

A soul contract with another person is not formed to make you happy or take care of you. There is a much deeper reason.

We come into this world with an agenda for our own growth. This agenda focuses on integrating our disowned parts. Let me explain what a disowned part is.

Have you ever been told that you are made 'in the image of God'? That means you are a perfect reflection of the state of eternal Love.

Then why are there so much strife, division and negativity in this world?

The reason is that **we disown parts of ourselves**. The result is an imbalance, where we own some of who we are, but also disown some of who we are.

Now this may be a new way of thinking for you, but just go with it for the moment.

You are on an eternal journey towards wholeness. The purpose of your existence here on earth and your soul contract with people is to experience specific aspects of yourself where you have never experienced wholeness before.

Let's say for example that you have never (not even in previous lives) honored and respected yourself. You enter into this life with the agenda of learning to honor and respect yourself. You have soul contracts with specific people who will assist you with this journey.

As you get on with your life, things start to 'go wrong'. For example, you are abused (physically or emotionally) by a parent. You marry a bully who does not value you as a person. You experience bullying at work. You fall into a deep pit of self-pity while more and more experiences just confirm to you that you are worthless.

Or do they?

What if every experience is designed to teach you that your self-worth does not come from other people, but from inside of you?

The people we deal with just confirm what our conversations, attitudes, body language, and other clues tell them about us.

Think about this: You have not seen a friend for a while. When the friend's name is mentioned, you recall a lively, bubbly pal with a zest for life. You remind yourself to give the friend a call, but before you get round to doing that, you encounter this friend while you are out shopping. The friend is very happy to see you, and still ready with humorous quips. Their physical appearance has not really changed. You suggest meeting for a drink but the friend is suddenly in a hurry and 'will get back to you'.

You feel confused. If you had a checklist of things that you recall about this friend, you would still, from this encounter, tick all the blocks. However, at the same time there is something you cannot quite put your finger on, and that something caused you to feel relief when your friend was not available for a drink. Was it the slight edge to the humor that made your hair raise for no specific reason? Was it the tiny line at the corner of their mouth? Was it the way the friend used their gestures, not to embrace the world as in the past, but rather to protect their core against the world?

This friend did not need to tell you anything about finding themselves in an abusive relationship and with loads of debts. The friend did not say in so many words 'I have lost my belief in myself. I am confused about the decisions I made that turned into nightmares'. You did not need to hear the details. You walk away from this encounter feeling relieved that you can walk away, and at the same time concerned about your friend – but not concerned enough to turn back and say 'Can I help you? I feel that you need a friend at the moment.'

Now place yourself into the shoes of your friend. They walk away thinking 'Here I am, feeling very alone in the world, and this so-called 'friend' is looking down on me. How dare they judge me? What did I do to deserve them looking down their nose at me?'

Can you see how much happened during this encounter? The friend has certain beliefs about themselves. You do not even know consciously what those beliefs are. You just observed very subtle clues and responded to those clues. Your behavior reinforced the beliefs of your friend, because they invited reinforcement.

We seldom learn to identify our soul agenda. We often focus on a one-sided perspective because we cannot see the wood for the trees.

This book teaches you to recall that soul agenda. **Once you understand what the purpose of the relationship is, you will be able to gain the wisdom that the relationship was designed to teach you.** You will integrate your dis-owned parts much faster and let go of the relationship.

We have soul contracts with specific people who help us experience the parts of ourselves that we dis-own. They continuously behave in a way that shows us these dis-owned parts until we own these parts with gratitude.

 Who do you believe you have a soul contract with?

Let me give you an example. You are in a relationship with someone who often lies to you.

Initially you find reasons to explain the lies away. When you run out of reasons, you start blaming yourself for the person's lies.

Over time you realize that nothing you do changes the situation – the person lies to you and to other people, regardless of how you behave.

Then you develop a revulsion in and distrust of this person. You feel you can no longer believe anything they say.

This situation has a serious impact on your relationship and the emotional distance between the two of you grows until you feel there is no relationship left.

As far as you are concerned, the problem with the relationship is your partner's lack of honesty.

Eventually your partner tells one lie too many, and you decide to end the relationship because you are 'not like that' – you don't tell lies.

Or you feel unable to end the relationship for various reasons, and you stay in the relationship on your terms, even though you are very unhappy.

When anyone asks you how you are, you put on a brave face and say 'I'm fine', even though you know you are falling apart. Are you telling the truth here?

When you take a step back, you realize that all people at some point tell lies – you included.

Does that make you a bad person, or a liar like your partner?

At this point you discover that life is a combination of shades of the truth. You realize that people present their version of the truth to the world. You do that as well.

You then take a step back and ask yourself why your version and your partner's version of the relationship are so different.

This is where your real growth and healing commence – when you begin to discover what is really important to you. You discover what you value, and what your partner values. You look beyond the lies and discover your own truth.

People hold up a mirror to us, as if they are saying to us 'Look at me. I am part of you. I am you. You might not love me, but I am still part of you.'

Our response is often to say 'I am not like that. I will do everything to distance myself from you, and I want you out of my face – and out of my life'

Various people could treat us in more or less the same manner until we 'get the message' and then find gratitude for their role in our process of self-discovery.

That is what this process is about – recognizing the role that people play in our lives, and recognizing their part in our personal journey of self-discovery and becoming whole.

The purpose of any relationship is to help us recognize the 'missing bits', in other words the parts that we say we do not have. Over time we accept these dis-owned parts as part of ourselves, and then love ourselves because we have grasped the value of those 'missing bits' and become whole as a result.

 What would you say is the biggest problem with your relationship? Don't think too much about the answer.

A relationship does not add anything to you.

The purpose of a relationship is to help you to understand that you already are and have everything.

As long as you do not understand this, you have a picture of an ideal relationship on the one hand, and you have reality on the other hand. **The bigger the difference is between your ideal and your reality, the more the emotional pain you experience in the relationship.**

All your soul contracts focus on the recognition of parts of you that you dis-own.

You are saying but there are people that you always have a good relationship with? Really? Is there even one relationship where you have never experienced any irritation, emotional reaction or disillusionment?

When you begin to look at relationships in terms of what they are meant to teach you about yourself, you get another step closer to self-love.

Some religious beliefs go against self-love – for example where self-love is described as vanity. However, those same religions describe you as an image of God and your body as a temple of God. You are also taught to love your neighbor like you love yourself. Have you ever questioned these discrepancies?

 Go through the list of reasons why your relationship has failed. Which of those reasons that you have attributed to others do in fact apply to you as well?

 Draw three columns on a sheet of paper. Use the following three column headings:

- **What my partner did wrong**

- **What other people did wrong**

- **Where I did the same thing, because at some level 'I am like that'**

List here the things that your partner or other people do or did which made you react by saying 'The relationship failed because I am not like that'.

Use an extra sheet of paper if necessary. And this exercise does not mean that you are breaking yourself down - on the contrary. As you do the exercise, you will feel what physically happens in your body and with your emotions.

In chapter 2 we will discuss how a relationship works.

Chapter 2: The Mechanics of a Relationship

In this chapter you will learn:

- Why you were born with 'temporary amnesia'
- How to get rid of the 'temporary amnesia'
- The three steps in resolving the emotions in your relationship

How does a relationship help you integrate your dis-owned parts and move closer to wholeness?

Remember, when we come into this world we do not arrive with a manual for life. We have our soul contracts, but we are born with what I like to describe as 'temporary amnesia'. For a long time we have no conscious knowledge of these soul contracts.

How Do We Get Rid Of The 'Temporary Amnesia'?

Imagine that your brain acts like a radio receiver, picking up radio waves from some transmitter outside of the earth.

As with a radio station, when you are on the correct wavelength, the reception is crystal clear. The message you receive relates to Love and forgiveness. And please put aside all your preconceived ideas about what Love and forgiveness mean. In this book we redefine both concepts to get back to the original meaning – as it is being transmitted from the Source.

Also, as with a radio station, when you are close but not on the correct wavelength, there is 'white noise' in the way. We gather our own 'white noise' from the moment we are born.

How do we gather 'white noise'? This happens when we learn specific responses to situations and gather preconceived ideas and prejudices along the way. We then remain stuck in those responses, ideas and prejudices until we have later life experiences where we are challenged to re-think everything.

We respond emotionally to everything that we experience, and we use our physical bodies to express those emotions.

For example, you know what makes you angry. You know what happens to your face and body when you become angry. You know the difference between your physical expressions of 'angry' and 'sad', because you get different clues for each of these emotions from your environment and you express the emotions in different physical ways using your face and body.

But how often do you step back and ask yourself why a specific trigger always makes you angry? Why does another trigger always make you sad? These triggers are quite personal – depending on your own past experiences and perceptions.

For example, you see a man chewing a piece of gum. How do you react?

- Do you not even notice it?

- Do you think 'I would like some gum'?

- Do you get irritated because an adult should know better than to chew gum – like your mother always said?

 What irritated you the most about your ex-partner?

Your answer will depend on your own perceptions and will be right for you.

Of course you can have multiple sets of emotions for the same set of information – and the physical expression of each of these emotions will differ. You can imagine the confusion you create in your body when you have many different emotions related to the same stimulus – much like driving a car and going in one direction only to discover a dead end and having to turn quickly before going over the edge, and at the same time watching out for other cars coming at you at full speed. That can only be exhausting!

For example you hear the front door open and you know it is your partner coming home for supper. He likes his routine and gets very angry if the food is not on the table. During the afternoon there was a power failure and the food is not ready yet.

The sound of the front door opening unleashes waves of guilt (because you are not a good wife), fear (because you know his temper), anger (because this is not your fault), and resentment (because you deserve to be treated well).

 How would you respond in such a situation?

Do you at this point take a step back and ask yourself which emotion is dominant? Do you ask what you need to learn from the situation about yourself?

Probably not. I would suspect that you forget to breathe, and that most of the muscles in your body tense up – and you prepare for fight or flight. And next time the same stimulus will result in the same response.

We intuitively know the purpose of all our experiences but we mask this purpose with our emotions.

Only when we clear away this 'white noise' do we move closer to the correct wavelength and intuitively receive pure information about ourselves.

As long as the 'white noise' is in place, we receive the information related to Love and forgiveness, but we mask that information with our emotions and we change it all around to confirm our own blockages.

For example, you intuitively know that your spouse should act with Love towards you, and in your mind they do this most of the time. Then you make a nasty comment about a person, and your spouse tells you the comment was unjustified. In your mind this confirms your suspicion that your spouse has a wandering eye, and off you go to accuse them that they no longer love you. You do not stop for a moment to ask yourself why you made the comment in the first place. You just assume that your spouse must love you unconditionally and you never even realize that you are the one adding the condition to their love.

 What conditions did you add to your relationship without realizing it?

When dealing with any issue in a relationship, we go through a three-step process. Where this process is not completed, we remain stuck on one of the three steps. This causes intense emotions and increased stress levels.

The three steps are explained below:

Step 1: Acknowledge Your Emotions

We all experience negative emotions. Where we do not want to acknowledge and own these negative emotions, one of two things happen.

- **We feel guilty for having these negative emotions.**

  There is an entire positive thinking industry that wants us to feel like failures whenever we have negative emotions or experiences.

  The leaders of this positive thinking industry have gardens with plants that die and re-grow. They cannot prevent the plants from dying. They also cannot prevent sunsets, droughts or floods.

  The Universe, the world and nature at every level is balanced. For every positive emotion we experience, there is a negative counterpart. If we do not acknowledge these negative emotions, they become more prominent until they overtake the positive emotions and there is no balance.

  When we accept both positive and negative emotions, we no longer list only guilt for failing to be positive on the negative side. We also no longer list only positive thinking and deny the darker realities of life.

  Recognizing all emotions without first judging them as either positive or negative is a significant first step in gaining from any relationship.

- **We deny the emotions, hoping that they will go away.**

  Some people regard emotions as a sign of weakness. As a result they suppress their emotions. This has the same effect as sweeping dirt under a carpet. This is a solution up to a point, when the dust pile gets too big to ignore. Then you keep tripping over the hump in the carpet, and you blame the carpet for being there. Who put the carpet there? Who swept the dust under the carpet?

We are meant to use our relationships so that we can acknowledge our emotions and neutralize them.

 What are your strongest emotions about your relationship?

Step 2: Question the Source of the Emotion

We have expectations that we want others to live up to. When our expectations are not met, we react with emotion.

Our expectations are based on

- **Our interpretations of our experiences.**

  These expectations are always one-sided because we are not taught to look for the other side. For example, you want a partner who is totally focused on you, so that you will never feel neglected like some of your friends do.

  Then you get such a partner, and what happens? Soon you feel smothered and want your own space. You blame your partner for taking up too much of your time and neglecting your friends and family. You chose the experience, but you focused on one side of the experience and denied the other side.

- **What our parents teach us.**

  In our early years we absorb everything we are taught without questioning. Later in life we discover that many of the things our parents taught us are no longer useful or stopped making sense. This creates conflict, because we want to use more appropriate responses to situations without being disloyal to our parents.

  For example, your parents married young and your mother always says that you must make a marriage work, no matter what, because people marry for life. Their marriage, on the surface, looks solid until you discover that your father has been having an affair for years. You tell your mother about this, and her response is that it is none of your business, and you must focus on keeping your own alcoholic husband happy.

Now you have a choice. Do you stay loyal to what your parents told you, or do you make up your own mind?

 What were your expectations of your relationship?

Step 3: Find the Hidden Side

Ask yourself these questions about the emotions that are triggered by your relationship:

- **Which of your values were offended?** For example, you value some time for yourself, but your spouse expects to have your attention all the time.

- **Which of your expectations were not met?** For example, you got married to have the perfect family, which includes one son and one daughter. Now you are a parent of four. The demands are too much for you, and your spouse is very happy to be the proud parent but leaves the physical work and discipline to you.

- **What did you feel entitled to that you did not get?** For example, you add your entire income to the household income. You have given up trying to convince your spouse that it is only fair that you both contribute equal percentages of your income and keep some pocket money for yourself.

- **What pay-off do you get for getting angry and being louder or tougher or stronger?** For example, when you lose your temper, is the reconciliation sex afterwards always better than ever?

- **Do you use anger to avoid taking responsibility?** For example, if your spouse knows that you get angry whenever the topic of credit cards is raised, do they remain quiet about your expenses to avoid your temper, and do you get away with that?

- **What is it in the other person's behavior that you feel angry about?** For example, does he always leave the toilet seat up, and do you feel he does it to provoke you?

- **What rule that you made was broken by the other person?** For example, did you decide that your children must always ask permission to have friends over, because it is convenient for you? Did your spouse then decide that you are too rigid and encourage your children to bring their friends any time?

- **How is the other person challenging you?** For example, do you prefer some domestic chaos, but your spouse always comments on your sloppy habits and inability to find things?

- **Are you holding a grudge that you need to let go of?** For example, do you feel that all men are unreliable because your father deserted you and your mother, and now your spouse constantly lives with your suspicion and jealousy purely because he is male?

- **What do you want from the other person?** Do you want your spouse to make you happy because nothing you do takes away that feeling of being inadequate?

- **What is the bigger picture?** Do you react on
    - Guilt (I did something bad, even if it was before I started this relationship, and I do not want to be discovered)
    - Shame (I am bad, because my parents always referred to me as 'the dark one in the family', even though I do not quite understand why, but they must be right)

- o Fear (I am vulnerable, and will do anything to get protection from my spouse or anyone else)
- **What is your inner conversation?** What do you keep saying to keep your anger raging?

 Which of the above questions relate to you and why?

We use our emotions to twist and turn the message from the Source into something that will fit our one-sided reality.

This is a painful process because it means swimming against the tide all the time. The pain increases when we realize that our version of reality is not as water-tight or correct as we thought it was.

Where we persist with only recognizing one side of the reality, our infatuation eventually turns into disillusion. Where we acknowledge the other side of the reality as well, we gain balance.

Every situation has an upside as well as a downside. When we want a perfect relationship, we deny the moments of disappointment until they grow out of proportion. When we have an unhappy relationship, we do not even bother to recognize the good parts of the relationship, because we focus on the bad parts only.

The outcome of the three steps above is that we complete a growth spiral (more about that in chapter 3) and become whole.

For example, you enjoy routine. You have a relationship with a person who is not disciplined, and a large part of the attraction for you is that your partner is your opposite.

Then you have a child. You want to ensure the child learns discipline, and your partner feels you are too strict. Over a period of time the tension increases, until it reaches breaking point.

You exchange harsh words – you because you cannot stand a lack of discipline, and your partner because they believe you are a control freak.

You part ways.

You then raise your child as a single parent. Of course you apply even more discipline, because you want to succeed with this task. When your child visits your ex-partner, there is no discipline, and this increases your irritation every time. As a result you have more rules and your poor child suffers in this tug-of-war.

Now take a step back. Of course we all need discipline. Of course we all need freedom. What if you and your ex-partner are both wrong? What if you are too disciplined and your ex-partner is too free?

How about trusting your child to choose what they feel comfortable with? If you understand that freedom without discipline results in disintegration and discipline without freedom is stifling, you become disciplined not for the sake of being disciplined, but because you want to enjoy the freedom of a casual routine.

 What did you and your ex-partner differ about to the extent that you argued about it on more than one occasion?

When you see both sides of the coin, you are no longer stressed out. You accept that your ex-partner will over time gain their own wisdom. You continue with your routine and discipline. When your child returns from a visit and objects to your routine, you don't need to be forceful because 'those people have no self-control'. You can welcome your child back into a familiar routine without stifling them.

Over time the child will find their own balance between self-discipline and spontaneity. As a result you will be more relaxed and find the same balance.

When you gain this insight, you own your need for routine as well as your need for spontaneity. You no longer judge others as being unruly, and you no longer deny your own unruly – or spontaneous - side.

The result is less tension and more acceptance - without letting go of the value you attach to routine and discipline.

Long-Term and Short-Term Relationships

Where two people enter into a long-term relationship (either romantic, friendship or family) the relationship is more complex. There are more agendas in a long-term relationship.

For example, parents have a relationship with each other and with their child for as long as they live.

The parents have joint challenges where they have to share their views about raising a child, or at least compromise on those views.

The parents also have separate challenges in terms of their relationship with each other as a couple.

In the next chapter we discover how the emotions resulting from a relationship are turned into feelings.

Chapter 3: Your Emotional Cycles

In this chapter you will learn:

- The importance of noticing patterns and cycles in your life.

- How your life consists of a series of spirals.

- What happens when you deal with your spirals.

- What gratitude really means.

You understand your life's purpose better when you identify patterns causing discomfort to you, and deal with those patterns. When you look back at your life, you can identify a number of situations where you had to wrestle with issues. Some of these issues would have involved other people, while others were more about yourself and your own belief systems.

Your emotions around these issues often get quite intense before they are resolved. Once the issue is resolved, you look back at it and at that point discover the wisdom that you have gained from the experience. This pattern brings insight and acceptance, and takes you to gratitude based on pure Love.

Once you can identify these cycles and patterns, you can process them so much quicker. You will no longer get despondent when the experience and your emotions get very intense, or when you realize that you have yet another issue that is building up.

You will be much more patient with yourself when you know why you feel intense emotions, or why there is always some issue in your life that needs resolution.

You learn to look forward to the feeling you get when resolving an issue. You appreciate feeling a sense of achievement when the issue is no longer there.

How do you recognize your life issues?

Think back of a time when you were content with your life. Before that time you had struggled with one or two issues, but in the end they were resolved and everything was going smoothly. You woke up with a zest for life, ready to start your day.

But then you had some concern. At first it seemed irrelevant, for example a chance comment you overheard, or an isolated, meaningless incident. Or it may have been something bigger, such as having some concerns regarding getting married, but deciding to work hard on your relationship. You were at the beginning of the emotional issue.

For various reasons your little concern grew over time. You often thought about it. You may even have experienced some health issues like stress because of this unresolved issue. It was like walking up the coils of a spiral, and it was hard work, walking uphill.

It felt like everything related to this issue just got worse and worse, until at some point you threw your hands up and said to yourself 'I cannot deal with this. It has got to end at some point. There must be more to life than this. This is too much for me.' It was as if the coils of the spiral became narrower the more you progressed. You felt like you were chasing your own tail. You experienced intense emotions and lots of inner pain.

Then somehow you had a resolution and heaved a sigh of relief. Your life became so much easier. You found joy again, looked back on those resolved issues, felt gratitude and moved on. You had reached the pinnacle of your spiral.

Have you identified at least one of your completed issues?

Try this exercise: Close your eyes and remind yourself of a very difficult situation that you managed to resolve successfully. This could be any situation where you felt quite stressed, but eventually it was all resolved.

Now imagine yourself at the most difficult point in the situation, standing on a coil near the top of the spiral, looking down.

Can you see the wide spiral coils below you?

Look up and notice how the coils of the spiral narrow to form a pinnacle. Why were you on this spiral?

Now write down some details of your completed experience. Identify

- **Your starting point. What triggered the situation? Was it one incident or a series of events?**

- **Those times where you could feel your turmoil intensifying. What made the whole situation worse? Can you recall how you felt physically? And emotionally? Can you recall your state of mind?**

The resolution. What was the wisdom or insight that brought you to a moment of gratitude and resolution?

Small Miracles

To understand what happens with our emotions we need to venture into the fields of physics and quantum mechanics – but I promise I will keep it simple.

When the atom was first discovered, it was thought to be shaped like a billiard ball. As science progressed, it was discovered that an atom was in fact not solid, but combined protons and electrons, with neutrons orbiting round this core.

However, this still didn't explain all atom behavior. Scientists discovered their own behavior impacted on the behavior of those atoms they were observing. This led them to the discovery of consciousness and the wave-particle theory, which describes all energy existing as waves. When you on purpose look for a specific form of energy, an energy wave becomes a particle.

For example, you decide you want to buy a new car, but you are not yet clear on exactly which make and model you want. From that moment on, you start to notice various cars and your elimination process begins. The waves of information around you turn into particles because you go looking for the information. Then you make your decision and you buy a specific car that meets all your requirements.

The same happens with a relationship. You have a memory of your soul contract, even though you might not even be aware of the memory or its contents.

When the time comes to implement this soul contract, you consciously start looking out for your partner. You may think that you are just dating, but in fact on an unconscious level you are looking for your contractual partner. This process may take a while and may involve other people as well. For example you may date a number of people and reject each one of them for a good reason, but you have soul contracts even with those people. Then you meet Mr. or Mrs. Right and a major spiral or emotional experience commences.

Of course this process is not the same for everyone. There are as many variations as there are people, for example 'chance meetings' that result in marriage, love at first sight, or even arranged marriages in some cultures.

 What is the most romantic real-life story you have ever heard?

All this forms part of a chemical process at cellular level in your body, where fermions turn into bosons.

Fermions

Protons and electrons are both fermions, or matter. That means you can touch them and observe them, even though they are minutely small. Fermions have been described as the building blocks of our Universe. Just like a selfish person, a solitary, unsociable fermion resists other fermions and as a result remains unbalanced and selfish. A fermion prides itself on being different from anything else ('I am different from others'), and because it pushes other fermions away, it remains solitary.

Each fermion needs its own space, and at any given time only one fermion can occupy any space (just like only one person can stand on any marked spot or sit on a chair). These rigid, stiff fermions reject interaction with other fermions, and as a result they don't grow but remain stationary and in a state of tension. For example, if there is only one comfortable chair to sit in while watching television, one person can sit in the chair. However, a number of people can argue about the chair until one person wins.

The fermions represent the part of you that you dis-own, as well as the opposite part that you own.

For example, if you claim that you are always honest, then you dis-own the part of you that sometimes tells little white lies or become overly tactful to protect people.

To put it bluntly, the liar and the honest person in you would both be fermions, one with a positive charge and one with a negative charge. The honest person in you will do everything to push away the liar, and will keep shouting 'I am not like that'. At the same time the liar in you will shout 'Do not deny me, or I will make things worse for you.'

The honest person and the liar in you will fight as hard as they can to claim the top spot for themselves. That will cause tremendous tension for you. There will be more and more situations where you have to choose between the truth and a lie, or where people deliberately lie to you and you then reject them because you are 'not like that'.

 Do you recognize yourself in the above description?

Bosons

At some point you will recognize that you are both an honest person and a liar. You will see how damaging honesty can be on occasion, and you will see how useful a lie can be at times. Or you may be the one who always lies and eventually you have to confront the truth, no matter how painful it is for you.

At this point of realization the fermions both give up tot battle for the top spot, while at the same time they both achieve the top spot and merge into one.

When fermions combine and work together, they act like bosons. They become force carriers rather than occupiers of space. A boson, consisting of an even number of fermions, is completely balanced. The boson is always happy to share and merge with others, with not even a hint of selfishness. Unlike the solid, selfish fermion, a boson is more like a ghost, and prefers to share rather than remain separate.

Because a boson is not solid, it knows no barriers. Nothing can stop it, and it carries a force that produces movement and radiation. This is how a boson lights the path for others to follow. A boson also knows no time or space.

Which opposites have you come to accept as both true over the years?

Time and Space

Why do you need to understand how fermions and bosons work?

You live on earth like a fermion. You believe your life experience is unique. When you go through a difficult phase in your relationship, you feel that nobody understands you. You like to reflect on your past and identify where you 'went wrong'. You think how things could have been different 'if only . . . '. You dread your future, and when your future becomes your present, you do not acknowledge your present to be far less dreadful than you imagined.

When you act like a boson, on the other hand, you lose all awareness of space and time. You become one in Love with those around you, and know no limitations to your creativity.

The more you gain control over your emotions, the more you gain a different perspective on your relationship and your life. You find those parts of your life where you have inner conflict. You receive intuitive guidelines on how to heal that inner conflict. You choose when to stop acting like a fermion (focusing on me, myself and I) and start acting like a boson (completely integrated and highly creative).

You might be wondering how you, as a human being, can lose all awareness of time and space. That is easy. I bet you do it often without even realizing it.

Do you ever daydream? When you do that, what space do you go to? Or does your daydream take place where there is no space? And while you are living that daydream, do you keep track of the time passing? Or do you discover later on how much time actually passed while you were visiting a dimension where time and space do not exist?

Imagine being able to take all your problems to that place where your daydreams happen. You will be able to quickly find a solution for all your problems, no matter what the nature of the problem is. That is not impossible at all. You only need awareness and some practice.

Quantum Leaps

The behavior of fermions and bosons also explain your behavior when you move up your spiral of strong emotional issues. You start at the bottom of your spiral, happy from resolving a previous emotional issue, but your life is never without any issues – that is why you live on this earth.

Over time, through incidents and situations, you become aware of something else that needs resolving. For example, an unhappy relationship doesn't become unhappy overnight. There is a series of incidents and issues that remind you of the need to resolve some inner conflict.

The fermions in your body reflect this division in your spirit. Your fermions want to remain separate and divided, no matter how much it hurts you. You want to hold on to that inner conflict, because you want one side to win – even if you are not always sure which side should win. As a situation spirals out of control, your inner conflict increases. This causes discomfort, and your irritation, anger, anxiety, feeling of powerlessness or other strong emotions increase.

 When was the last time that you felt completely stressed out? What was it about?

Then the two sides of the inner conflict merge and you realize the wisdom that you needed to gain from the situation. In that moment you lose all sense of time and space. Boundaries crumble and you release your pent-up tension. A boson forms in a moment of immense gratitude, where your heart opens up and you experience true Love.

Remember how the stress was resolved? How did you feel?

Gratitude

You gain a glimpse of unconditional Love while you experience gratitude. This only lasts for a fleeting moment in eternity, because when the moment passes you at once attach conditions again and forget about true Love.

If you have a child, think of when you first held them in your arms. Your heart opened up like a lotus flower and you experienced indescribable joy. You had a quick glimpse into eternity and your journey's purpose.

After your eternal moment had passed, your expectations of your child started. You waited for their first smile or first tooth, and compared them with children their age, to confirm 'normality'. You applied conditional love again.

You probably experienced a moment of gratitude and unconditional Love when your partner first declared their love for you, or when you felt quite close to a friend or a relative. Once your moment had passed you felt conditional Love again.

These moments of gratitude reflect a completed spiritual spiral, where an inner conflict resolves and you experience a quantum of light in every cell of your body.

After this experience your entire body vibrates at a higher level. You have a life-long memory of your gratitude, which becomes part of your eternal memories. When you experience gratitude, your inner conflict heals and you remember your eternal roots. Once you have experienced gratitude and true Love, you will do anything to experience similar moments.

If you don't reach a moment of gratitude and true Love, you continue to feel frustration and regret for what you didn't achieve, or resentment for other people's actions. However, when you focus on working towards moments of gratitude, your awareness expands with every experience. You become much more aware of your emotions, and with the resolution of each inner conflict you feel lighter and more whole.

How Can I Feel Gratitude for Ending a Relationship?

You may ask what all this has to do with ending your relationship? I am sure you would agree this single event has impacted on your emotional, physical, spiritual, financial and social life. When you realized that your relationship has in fact ended, you became aware of a massive inner conflict consisting of a number of smaller conflicts.

When you understand your experiences and your emotional and physical reactions to your world, you will feel gratitude and know you have become a little bit more whole.

Recognizing this healing process will help you re-live 'good' memories and discover your unrecognized life lessons from 'bad' memories. You will feel a physical and emotional difference when you recognize new opportunities. You will resolve your physical tension as your spiritual tension resolves.

There have been moments since you became disillusioned with your relationship where you experienced a light, floating, peaceful feeling. Remember those moments where you knew you had courage to go on? They may have been as a result of small incidents or moments with people where you felt gratitude. For some people those moments may have been few and far between, but they were there.

 Note down your moments of gratitude, no matter how small they were. By doing this, you become awareness of each inner conflict that gets resolved. You get to recognize true gratitude and acknowledge your own journey towards wholeness, even with baby steps.

Your next list will perhaps be much longer than your list of moments of gratitude. Before you even

begin your list, promise me you won't feel guilty or judge yourself or resent those people you think of. This is a list of work to be done, not a guilt trip.

Imagine yourself being an observer of your own life. Consider those emotions you feel most often, and want to have less of. Think of people making your life harder or more complicated with their attempts to help you. Remember those irritating people, or those you feel rejected by. Also think of everything that makes you feel unable to control your life, such as having to pay bills when this was your partner's job, dealing with teachers with no comprehension of what you and your children experience, being unable to dine out on your own and so on.

Note down as many as possible of these emotions, people and circumstances you don't feel grateful for right now. List your issues without punishing yourself.

Having a long list doesn't make you ungrateful for what you have. It means you have courage to acknowledge those issues you recognize as part of your own inner conflict.

What Will Happen When You Resolve Your Current Inner Conflict?

Will you ever resolve an inner conflict and not have conflict again? Yes, but not in your lifetime.

The resolution of inner conflict follows a spiral, a sacred geometric shape providing you with a glimpse of eternity. With every spiral you complete, you become more whole and integrated. Little by little you gain perspective on those troublesome issues in your life, and you realise how each one of them become irrelevant once you have gained the wisdom. You notice your bigger picture.

Does your journey become easier? Yes, it does. Every inner conflict that you resolve makes you stronger and equips you for your next challenge. In a manner of speaking, your spiritual legs become stronger and you become fitter, and as a result your climb becomes easier.

You recognize those moments when part of you has made a quantum leap from being a fermion to becoming a boson. Every time it happens, your body is more relaxed, you vibrate at a higher level, and you become less prone to dis-ease.

With every inner conflict you resolve, you also feel more comfortable in your own skin. People notice this and they respond to you by reflecting more Love to you.

Situations and themes tend to repeat until you have the insight and resolve that inner conflict. These situations do not only relate to one specific relationship. For example, if you are in a relationship where your partner cheats, you may find that people at work and friends also cheat on you.

You may be tempted to believe that all people cheat and you cannot trust anyone. Of course that is true – we all cheat someone at some point in our life.

However, you will only resolve your inner conflict and become a complete person when you see the other side of the coin – when those two opposite fermions stop fighting against each other and melt together to form a boson.

When and how will that happen?

You will only gain the wisdom and complete the spiral when you recognize and own the other side of the equation.

For example, what did you need to learn about yourself from a cheating partner or friend or colleague?

Suppose you have planned that specific lesson because you needed to discover what makes a person unique. People may cheat you because you make assumptions about what is important for them and you never confirm your assumptions. They do not have the words or the courage to tell you what is important to them.

For example, you insist on having the full attention of your partner as proof of his dedication to you. You resent every minute he spends watching or participating in sports, because when he does that, he spends time with people that you do not like.

Your partner initially accepts that you want him to stay away from his sporting pals, but over time he realizes that he wants to spend equal time with you and with his other passion, which is sport. He knows that you will disapprove of his sporting activities, and he does not have the words to express what he wants.

He starts to see his sporting pals behind your back. Initially he just indulges in his passion for sports, but then he meets a woman who shares his passion for sports.

Eventually you discover his affair, but you still deny his passion for sports. He will not change, and neither will you. Do you accept his uniqueness and your uniqueness? Or do you fixate on the affair and blame him for his behavior? What if you take the opportunity to clarify what is really important for you, and then thank your partner for helping you discover that?

Let's say that you realize your need for his full attention is because you feel very insecure. Whenever you do not have his full attention, you are unconsciously reminded of the times when your parents left you with an unpleasant child minder. Even when you said that you would rather be with them, they did not understand what you wanted. Since then you have felt abandoned, and you have expected lots of attention from other people to take away that feeling of loneliness, with no success.

Now you can look back and realize that as a result of the way your parents acted, you had to cope with this child minder. This person was unkind to you on many occasions, and as a result you realized the importance of treating others with kindness. You never thought to thank this nasty child minder for this wisdom, because you remain focused on the idea that your parents abandoned you, even though you are the only one who saw it like that.

As a result of your partner's affair, you had to resolve this fear of being abandoned, and you realized that you were in fact never abandoned by anyone.

When you realize this wisdom, you will not only get to know yourself. You will experience a moment of gratitude. You will be able to thank your partner for what he helped you realize. Then you will be able to indulge in your own passions without expecting someone else to change and comply with your fantasy. You will no longer want other people to make you feel important or loved, because you will notice the kindness that you show towards other people, and be kind to yourself as well.

And if that is the end of the relationship? Then the relationship has served its purpose and it is time for you to move on.

It is also possible that behavior you perceive as cheating in fact points to another wisdom, where you deny your partner's needs because they do not fit in with your fantasy.

What if you had expectations that your partner did not meet? You are still stuck with the expectations and you still insist on your partner behaving in a way that was never natural for them.

For example, you and your partner are both ambitious. You both want to achieve the best in your live. You both work very hard to realize your objectives – so hard that you stop communicating. Then one day you discover that your partner is cheating on you.

Of course you respond emotionally to the situation, because your fantasy of your ideal life is destroyed. You blame your partner for abandoning your dreams and getting involved with another person.

Their response is that it is your fault because you stopped noticing them. You were working so hard that you forgot your partner, or you assumed that they would remain the same person, while you changed and grew from your own challenges. They did not remain the same person. We all change and grow all the time – in some aspects together as a couple and in other aspects separately.

Your partner discovered that they value physical attention and communication. They did not get that from you. At the same time you discovered that you value career success and admiration from colleagues. You did not get that recognition from your partner.

Often the logical course of action is to start blaming each other for your failures. But what if you both grew and failed to notice each other's growth? What if you rather decide to honor each other's values and move on? What if that was what you needed to learn from each other?

As long as you insist on seeing only your side of the relationship, your pain will continue and the relationship will not end, even if you physically separate.

On top of that, the same message will be reflected in different relationships. You will discover that the same theme occurs in other relationships. The shop assistant will be distracted and give you too little change – she is cheating you! Your colleague will ensure that you get the lion's share of the work and they share the praise for your hard labor – he is cheating you!

When you start looking for the theme, it is easy enough to recognize what you have been dis-owning. Then the question is: do you blame others for the way they treat you, or do you do some introspection? Do you ask yourself where in your life you displayed the same behavior?

This is the most challenging and also the most enriching part. Let's stay with the theme of cheating. Can you recall all the instances in your life where you cheated? Can you recall this without judgment?

Cheating on a game of chess when you were at school is no different from cheating on your first boyfriend before you decided to leave him, or cheating in a marriage. We base our actions on our values. Even (and especially) when we cheat, we can justify our own behavior based on what is really important to us.

We always act in terms of what we value, and that brings us closer to true Love.

What do you value in your relationship? You can list the things that everyone believes should be valued, like honesty, or you can be honest and practical and list the things that are essential for you in your relationship.

For example, I value small gestures like someone lighting a candle or opening a door for me.   I value quiet time for myself to think and write.

 Make your own list here. Your values may include things that you already have that are not negotiable, or things that you are really missing.

Chapter 4: What is True Love?

In this chapter you will learn:

- What true Love really is

- How you can experience true Love more often.

- What happens when you experience true Love.

- What impact moments of true Love will have on your relationship.

- How true Love changes your physical body.

This chapter does not contain good news for romantic souls. True Love is a state of bliss, but it does not last for years. In fact it only lasts for a moment – and it is not even possible to measure the moment, because it is a moment beyond space and time.

This will need some explaining.

Refer to the previous chapter where you learned about the process of two fermions fighting each other until finally they merge and form a boson. That moment when the boson is formed, is an instance of true Love. That instance can in terms of time last anywhere from seconds to hours. During that window period, we experience our true Loving nature.

Then we get ready for the next emotional issue to resolve, and the next integration. We repeat this process from the day we are born until the day we die. Every time we resolve an emotional issue, our physical bodies change and we become lighter.

When we hold on to our prejudices, preconceived ideas and other barriers to the flow of energy, we slow down the integration process. We drag out the emotional experience until the inner conflict reaches breaking point. At the same time we put our bodies under immense pressure. Our bodies react to this pressure by expressing dis-ease.

 If you have a physical ailment, think back to when you first became aware of the symptoms. What happened in your life at the time? What emotions did you experience?

The emotions are only resolved when we experience a moment of true Love and become aware of the wisdom we gained from the experience.

We can go through agony until we finally experience that moment in the course of events, and that could take a very long time. On the other hand, we can consciously work towards understanding the nature and purpose of the inner conflict and experience the moments of gratitude much quicker and more often.

When you consciously work on the process, it does not mean that the moment of gratitude or true Love is worth less. It simply means that you truly become the master of your own destiny in a loving way and you finally understand and realize the purpose of your relationship.

This is the only way to end a relationship and gain on a permanent basis.

And what about your partner? Will it make any difference if you consciously work on this process and achieve your results, but your partner does not do the same work? Will your partner gain from this process?

Yes, your partner is affected as well – both directly and indirectly.

The direct impact is that your own level of energy increases. The vibration of the energy that you radiate changes and the world perceives you in a different way. Your partner's perception of you also changes, based on their values and expectations.

Imagine throwing a stone into water. See the concentric circles emanating from the spot where the stone hit the water. That is want you do with your body all the time.

Now imagine throwing two stones of equal size into the same water. There will be concentric circles emanating from the impact of both stones. These circles will clash and cause waves. This is similar to what happens when you and your partner both are emotional and you have conflict.

Now imagine throwing a large stone and a small stone into the same water. There will still be concentric circles emanating from both stones, but the waves from the larger stone will overwhelm the waves from the smaller stone. When you achieve that moment of gratitude and your vibration increases, you become the 'larger stone' and your stronger vibration of Love energy impacts on the people around you, including your partner.

Is it possible for your partner to become the 'larger stone', still full of anger and other negative emotions?

Let me ask another question: is it possible for you to cross your arms in self-defense and at the same time embrace the world with Love? Of course not. A higher vibration is always based on more Love and on embracing more of the world.

A lower vibration is always based on more fear and self-protection at the exclusion of the world.

The other impact for you is that you no longer act from a basis of fear, resentment or guilt. You understand why you have had the experience. You have consciously gained the wisdom, and you act from a basis of unconditional Love.

This of course means that the dynamic between you and your partner changes drastically. It is like being in the middle of a tango, and the music changes to a waltz. The only way you can stay together in a relationship is if your partner also begins to act from a basis of unconditional Love.

Of course there is a very good chance that your partner will not yet be ready to see the other side of their own coin and gain from ending the relationship. Remember, when you feel ready to move on, it is because you have completed your forgiveness process. You have gained your own wisdom, and that wisdom included a moment of unconditional Love for the person who shared the experience with you. Each person achieves that point at their own pace. If your partner is not ready yet, your role is to love them and at the same time get on with your life.

You do not do anyone a favor when you hold on to a relationship where you are ready to move on. If you hold on to a relationship because you feel pity for your partner, or because you feel that your partner will not be able to survive without you, you in fact hold back yourself as well as your partner. Your actions – or lack of actions – stifle your own growth because you stay in a relationship for the wrong reasons. You also stifle the growth of your partner, because you continue to take responsibility for them and delay their own learning experiences.

True Love and Sex

Does a loving relationship and good sex not mean that you have found true Love?

No, it means that you have found true contentment. It means that you have found someone who is sharing life experiences with you.

Unsatisfactory sex is an unresolved emotional issue in its own right. When there is conflict in the relationship, you become even more aware that your entire body is a sexual organ and receptor. When you are not fully involved in the sexual relationship, it is an indication that you and your partner are working on different emotional experiences.

In some relationships two people each have their own experiences to share. They often work against each other, because that is how they designed their life experiences. This often creates the impression of an 'unhappy' relationship – where we have a fantasy about how the perfect relationship will work but the reality looks quite different.

In other relationships two people share the same experiences – they do not work against each other, but rather live through the same experience together and learn together. When this happens, they still have their individual experiences, but they are joined together at soul level. This does not mean that they are experiencing true Love. This is still true contentment.

True Love is only a moment in eternity, and we experience those moments when we gain the wisdom and insight that an experience is meant to give us. This is a moment where your heart opens up and you see the entire Universe with everything in it for a fleeting moment. You feel an immense gratitude which leaves you floating somewhere beyond space and time. You have no emotions – only a feeling of immense lightness.

The awareness of this moment of true Love does not last, but the effect does last. In that moment when you experience true Love, the vibration of your entire physical body increases. You become more receptive of your environment and the people around you. You are left with an awareness of your own spirit and your true self. You spend the rest of your life working towards the next moment of awareness of true Love.

You are also left with the knowledge that another person has honored a soul contract with you. Once you have experienced that knowledge, even a person that you might have perceived as the greatest monster loses their power over you. You acknowledge the completion of the soul contract, and you see a person who is as human and fallible as you are.

You might even see that you spent years being afraid of an illusion that was created by a weak person. This is truly a moment where your eyes open and you see your tormentor in a different light. You see the weak side of someone who pretended that they only have a strong side, and who used that pretense to intimidate you. You experience a moment of true Love for your adversary.

After this moment of true Love, you discover that your outlook on life changes. You have empathy for the weak people that you encounter. You have no fear for anyone. You experience a Love for humanity that remains with you.

Does the experience of true Love mean that you no longer have challenges in your life? Of course not.

The experience of true Love is fleeting, but the result is permanent. Your energy vibration changes permanently to a higher level and it will never change back.

Your life challenges reflect this permanent change in you. The challenges get more complex and more personal. The conflict you experience is less between you and other people, and more within yourself.

For example, you could still have the occasional conflict with your in-laws. The difference is that whereas you initially experienced strong emotions, you now experience an unemotional sense of wanting to see how the puzzle of life fits together.

Life continues as it was before you experienced the moment of true Love, but you view this life in a different way. You look forward to the difficult patches, because you know what waits for you when the emotional issue resolves. This makes each difficult patch worth your while and because you know this, there is no longer a sting in your life challenges.

The next chapter describes how you can use your knowledge of spirals and true Love to end a relationship.

Chapter 5: How to End a Relationship

In this chapter you will learn:

- Why all relationships have a natural end.

- Why it is necessary to let go of a relationship when it has reached its natural end.

- The reasons why people hold on to relationships long after they have ended, and how to resolve those reasons.

- How to end a relationship with Love.

How Long Does a Relationship Last?

As with everything in nature, a relationship has a natural life cycle.

A relationship can last

- For a lifetime (for example a parent-child relationship)

- For years (for example a long marriage or friendship)

- For months (for example a part-time job)

- Even for minutes (for example when you pay a sales person in a shop for an item)

The reason why the relationship ends is that you have completed a natural process where two opposing parts of you needed to integrate and become one.

If you want to grow towards a higher state of wholeness, it is essential to complete the process that finally ends the relationship. Once you have ended the relationship at all levels and moved on, a void is created.

Yes, many people enter this void and feel lonely and unfulfilled. This is because they do not understand that you need to let go of the old so that you can make space for the new. When you do understand the process, you enter the void and understand that there will be a 'resting time' before you move on to the next phase of your life. This 'resting time' is essential for you to use to establish who you have become.

The void is also necessary so that you can fill it by starting on the next cycle of growth. If the void is not created, you stagnate in one space and you block the flow of energy in and around your body because you fear moving forward into the unknown. This energy block is experienced in physical symptoms of dis-ease.

Imagine an energy circuit running clockwise around your body, starting at your head, going down the left side of your body, and up the right side of your body. There is a similar energy circuit running anti-clockwise around your body.

There is also a line of energy running down your spine from the crown of your head, and another line of energy running up your spine to your crown.

When you hold on to a finished relationship for any reason, these energy flows are blocked somewhere along the line. Energy that cannot flow freely stagnates and is expressed as dis-ease in your body.

As long as you have unresolved issues about the relationship, the process will not complete and the energy blockage will continue. The more unresolved issues you have, the more painful the relationship will become.

What are unresolved issues?

Let me answer with a question. If you are in a relationship that you are not leaving, what is destroying you? What have you not been happy about for a long time? If you have the opportunity to end this relationship today, what will stop you?

What will prevent you from ending the relationship? When you start saying 'yes, but . . . ', you tell me about your unresolved issues.

Those issues are there because you have beliefs that prevent you from growing.

Let's have a closer look at some of those issues:

- My partner is too weak to live without me. They will do something irresponsible when I leave.

- I will not survive financially.

- We have been together for so long that I cannot imagine a life without them.

- I am unhappy and lonely, but I think it will be worse to be on my own.

 Add your concerns to the list.

Do you notice how each one of those concerns creates a future based on fear? This is a fear of the unknown, fear for survival, fear of many things that do not exist yet because you are still in the process of creating them.

The secret does not lie in removing the fear.

The secret lies in looking back at what you have gained from the relationship, and feeling gratitude for the Love that you are being shown.

People often 'end' a relationship by severing all visible ties. They get a divorce, stop contacting the ex-lover, and even move to a different part of the country.

However, as long as you have not completed that process and grasped the lesson, the invisible ties remain.

If you still recall a 'bad' relationship, it indicates that you have not completed the experience. You are still stuck with the physical and emotional results of being out of balance.

There is also still a strong spiritual bond between you and the person you had the 'bad' experience with.

If you read up about near death experiences, there are many descriptions of a silver cord that keeps your esoteric body (or spirit) attached to you physical body while you are in this life. This cord is severed when you die and leave your physical body behind.

When you have a relationship, there is a similar silver cord that ties you to the other person. This spiritual bond can be visualized as a silver cord running from the area around your navel to the area around the other person's navel.

The spiritual bond is only severed when you have fully grasped the wisdom that you needed to gain from your experience in the relationship. It can take years for this spiritual bond to be severed. While the bond is in place, you have 'bad' memories of the relationship or you are stuck in patterns that only you can break.

You will know that the bond is still in place when

- The other person appears in your dreams
- You have a physical and emotional reaction in the presence of this person

- You have an emotional reaction when you even think about this person.

- You know what you want to avoid in your current or future relationship based on your experience of a past relationship.

The issue that made you label an experience as 'bad' is the issue that you need to investigate until you find the growth experience for you.

 Draw two columns on a sheet of paper.

Call the first column 'This is what I want to leave behind from a past relationship.'

Call the second column 'This is what I have learned about myself from this past relationship.'

Now think about the relationship that you want to leave behind. What is it that you want to leave behind? What is it that you are steering clear of?

List those issues in the left hand column below.

Then indicate in the right hand column what you have learned about yourself by experiencing those issues.

We often hold on to a relationship when we do not know what to expect if we end the relationship – a case of 'better the devil you know than the devil you don't know'.

It is easier to let go of a relationship when we understand that the successful end of a relationship means

- The disappearance of emotional pain. When we face the obstacles and objections that we use to prevent the natural end of a relationship, we integrate the parts of ourselves that cause the emotional pain.

- Understanding that we create our own experiences. The energy you put into fearing the future and the unknown is the same energy you put into dreaming about and creating the future you want.

- Creating a void that can be filled with what we desire for ourselves.

- Holding on to what is familiar because it serves us rather than out of fear for the unknown.

- Gaining the wisdom that you were meant to realize from the relationship

Often ending a relationship is experienced as a staccato process, because we deal with one obstacle after another. It feels like you deal with one issue, and then the next issue appears, and then the next one. There is a reason for this.

An intimate relationship is always complex, because the nature of the relationship implies a number of emotions that we choose to resolve with our partner as participant.

Ending a relationship implies dealing with all the issues that we need to leave behind, as well as dealing with all the issues we create in relation to the future.

When you deal with one issue, your unconscious mind gets a signal that you are now ready to deal with a more complex issue, and that is why they are paraded out of the closet of your unconscious mind one after the other.

Where an ended relationship still evokes emotions such as regret and guilt over the past, resentment of the present and fear of the future, there are still uncompleted issues that you need to identify and complete.

These emotions indicate that the inner division that was caused by the relationship has not been resolved. Your growth is hampered and you are not ready to create a void before you move into the next growth phase.

There are people who leave behind more than one relationship with the same negative emotions. They often move into a next relationship with a different person but the same issues appear. If the person does not resolve the issue, then the same situation will appear over and over until they get the message and grasp the wisdom.

For example, a person who is emotionally abused in a relationship will probably experience the same emotional abuse at work and from relatives, until they grasp the fact that feeling good about yourself comes from how you perceive yourself. No other person can make you feel good about yourself. You may feel good about yourself in the presence of another person, but that will not last. The only consistent source of Love for yourself is inside of you, and that is often what bullies teach us – if we are willing to learn.

When you master the process and learn to face and complete these processes, the impact is instant. However, if you have already expressed the imbalance of uncompleted processes in the form of physical dis-ease, the visible impact may not be instant.

You need to change your mind to think in a specific way. With every process you complete, you change more of your thinking and more energy flows freely. This means that you first heal spiritually, then the emotions are gone, and then you see the physical signs of the healing of the dis-ease.

People always expect an immediate miracle, but it is not always possible to undo the programming of a lifetime in one moment. It is necessary to recognize every small step and every moment of lightness individually. If you do not recognize your progress and your wisdom, you trigger the same obstacles and boundaries and re-create them again.

On the other hand, if you do recognize your progress, your body responds and you become aware of the higher energy vibration in your body. This allows for the flow of energy to increase, and the process becomes iterative – in other words, more insight always results in even bigger insights.

The feeling when you resolve an emotion is a conscious recognition of both sides of the existing situation. You see the balance in the situation whereas before you chose to only see one side of the coin, namely the misery that you chose to get stuck in.

When you have completed the entire process, you have resolved all emotions and you have experienced the moment of true Love and gratitude, it is necessary to celebrate the end of the relationship.

This can be a physical celebration, or it can simply be a moment of gratitude when you put into words what you have gained from the experience.

There are even people who end a relationship with a 'divorce holiday' where they allow themselves to be open to each other about the successes and failures of the relationship, and to share what they have gained from each other.

If it is not possible to share the gratitude of ending a relationship with your partner, it is still possible to celebrate the end of a relationship without your partner.

There are times when one person completes the process and the other person still holds on for dear life. In these instances, the silver cord that ties the two people still gets cut. The one partner will move on and continue with their life, while the other partner will be like a lost soul, floating from one destructive situation to the next. These are the choices we make. We all know intuitively when it is time to let go, and we need to follow our intuition.

Where an ex-partner is like a lost soul, they have their own emotions to resolve in their own way and at their own pace. If we hold on to a relationship purely because we want to prevent a partner from becoming a 'lost soul', we hold back the growth of that partner and also our own growth. This would be like in protecting a child from all the consequences of their actions well into adulthood – all you do is raise a child who remains a child and never grows up. That is not what the relationship is about.

Chapter 6: What is Keeping You in the Relationship?

In this chapter you will learn:

- How emotions such as guilt, resentment, regret and fear tie you to a dead relationship

- How limiting beliefs prevent you from taking action.

- How you make assumptions about your future and then make those assumptions come true.

- How to end a relationship once and for all

People remain stuck in a finished relationship for different reasons. This chapter will deal with a number of reasons why people hold on to their relationship.

Guilt and Resentment

The first reason for holding on to a relationship is guilt from the past – or even about the past. You want to hold on to a person because you feel guilty about situations that have occurred, and you feel you owe it to your partner to stay in the relationship.

Here is something about guilt that you may not know. Guilt is a one-sided perception. And that one side of the perception is the side that you chose to see at the time.

Here is an example: you have been in a long relationship with someone. At some point the person was ill and needed to be hospitalized. At the same time you had a great opportunity at work that required all your attention.

You knew your partner needed your emotional support while in hospital, but you also knew that missing your opportunity would have a negative impact on your career. At that time ambition was more important to you, because you knew that your partner would get well. You decided to ensure your partner was settled in hospital, and asked some friends to help out by visiting the patient while you took care of work.

Your partner did not say anything at the time, but you knew the signs of disapproval and this was at the back of your mind while you focused on the work opportunity.

Then your partner was given a wrong prescription and had an allergic reaction. By the time you could tear yourself away from work, the worst was over at hospital and your partner was recovering.

Even though nothing was said between you, you clearly got the message that during a critical time you were not there for your partner.

At the time you unconsciously decided that you will never again abandon your partner when they are in emotional or physical pain, because they need you at these times. However, never is a very long time.

You had to live with that guilt for a long time, and towards the natural end of the relationship this guilt is becoming more pronounced.

This time round you decide to stay in a relationship that is clearly hurting both you and your partner, because you do not want to feel guilty about abandoning your partner during their crisis time again – and this time you are part of the cause of the crisis as well, so there are buckets full of guilt.

Now take a step back. Find the other, unacknowledged side of the coin.

Did you really stop giving your emotional support when you were absent from the hospital? Of course not. Even though you were involved in the work opportunity, your thoughts were with your partner most of the time. We have a spiritual connection to our partners that is not severed when we are physically apart.

Could you take responsibility for the wrong prescription or for your partner's allergic reaction? Of course not. If you were present, the prescription would still have been given, and they would still have had the allergic reaction. You may even have made the situation worse by having a strong emotional reaction and being in the way of the medical staff while they needed to apply emergency treatment.

Did you make many other decisions over the years because of one incident? Probably, and chances are you were not even aware of it at the time.

And now, at the end of the relationship, that guilt features in almost all your decisions, and it is crippling you. You can see how the guilt has become redundant, and you know you no longer have any use for the guilt. However, you also do not give yourself the freedom and the opportunity to scout for other means of making decisions or behaving.

In many other situations you can make appropriate decisions based on a choice of options. You know what the appropriate behavior would be, and if you are not sure, you weigh your options and then choose.

However, in terms of your relationship you are stuck in one way of thinking on the basis of a decision you did not even consciously make at the time.

There is another equally important side of this coin.

What did your physical absence mean to your partner? They lived, did they not? They managed to get through the crisis without your presence. They had to rely on their own inner resources and the resources were there.

At the time your partner may have chosen to resent your absence, and they formed a permanent decision to always resent your absence during a crisis, because they did not appreciate being forced to use their own inner resources. Was that your choice? Of course not. We each make our own decisions and we shape our lives based on those decisions.

What if you and your partner had a soul contract that you would build your life together for the purpose of teaching each other about relying on your inner resources and not having to take responsibility for someone else's life and decisions? And when you understand this and truly grasp the lesson, you can express gratitude towards your partner for participating in the lesson for the duration of the relationship.

On the other hand, if you just cling to the emotions rather than detach yourself from the situation, the pain of staying in a finished relationship becomes quite intense. As long as you hold on to an outdated decision for dear life, you use a lot of energy treading water. This is physically exhausting as well.

When you approach the end of a relationship, you need to identify the emotion that ties you to your partner. When you have the courage to ask that question, you will intuitively know where the emotion first surfaced and why.

That will enable you to find the other side – the benefit that you disowned at the time, or the drawback that you denied at the time.

What do you feel guilty about in your relationship? Should you still carry that guilt?

Regret

Of course it is possible that you do not have any guilt about the past. You only regret that your dream never worked out the way you imagined.

Too many people begin a relationship with a fantasy of eternal true love, a white wedding, a strong male and a fertile female. And yes, I know this is the 21st century, but people still experience the pressure of having to get married because that is the norm.

So you read all the books, and the two of you planned your lovely wedding in detail. On the day you had the entire fairytale and went on your well-planned holiday.

Then the cracks started appearing.

He does not put the toilet seat down. She spends too much money on shoes.

Having children is not as it is pictured in the magazines. Children bite and often stink and keep you awake at night, having no regard for your deadlines at work. He does not accept his share of the child care. She does not live up to the image of the yummy mummy and wants to get back to work because she is yearning for adult company and silence.

The dream is long gone. All that is left is the reality and the monthly bills as part of the reality check.

All the marriage counseling books and textbooks on relationships say that you need to do as much as you can to make the relationship work. Yes, touching each other is important. Regular, meaningful communication does resolve many misunderstandings. And I am sure you can add to the list of advice, tips and recipes that guarantees a long and happy relationship. But what if you tried all of those and you feel you are slowly dying inside? Does that mean you have to stay in the relationship?

That is for you to decide.

How do you make the decision? You find the other side of the coin.

I can hear you asking: what is the other side of the coin in a relationship that from the beginning never met my expectations? How can I find gratitude in looking at my shattered dreams?

Firstly, you can take my word that there is always another side, whether we recognize it or not. At microscopic level our bodies cannot function without both protons and electrons. Life on earth cannot continue without day and night. As a species we go through the cycle of birth and death. Can you imagine how we will exist with only life, or with only death?

Here is the question you need to ask to find the missing side of a failed fairy tale: what did you gain from the experience? How did the relationship change you into the person you have become? What wisdom did you gain from the relationship?

For example, before having the relationship you assumed everything in life was rosy. Now you know that every light side has a dark side, and you are much more realistic. You know that there are times when things get sticky, and you also know that those are the times when you learn most about yourself and experience most personal growth.

Before the relationship you had massive expectations of your partner to make you happy. As a result of the relationship you have realized that happiness does not come from another person, but from inside of you. But you had to first live through a hell of loneliness before you could understand that.

Before the relationship you did not have children. Now you know the joys (as well as the pain) of parenthood and that has made you more mature and much more resourceful.

When you add up all the ways in which you have changed, grown and become wiser as a result of the relationship, you will slowly realize that the relationship in fact did not fail, but succeeded in making you the person you are.

Of course some people only identify the dark side of the relationship. They will describe how they have become bitter, disillusioned, addicted to substances, resentful and so on. This means they have much work to do on discovering the light side which is inevitably there, but disowned by them.

Regret at the end of a relationship means not having identified everything you gained from the relationship. Every relationship is a means of enacting a soul contract. That soul contract happens for a reason, namely so that we can learn and grow and become more integrated at cellular level.

With regret often comes self-blame – where you feel you did not do enough to keep the relationship going.

Can you for a moment put the self-blame aside and look at the gains? When you have a balanced view of your relationship, you also get a different view on the reasons why you thought you should blame yourself.

Then there is the question of responsibility.

Who is responsible for your partner's physical and emotional well-being? You might be staying in a relationship because you are blackmailed by a partner who threatens to self-harm when the relationship ends. Or you may be in a relationship with a partner who is already self-harming, for example with an addiction.

But do you ever question who is responsible for your own behavior while you take responsibility for your partner's behavior? What if you block or deter your partner's emotional and spiritual growth by remaining in a relationship and continuing to accept responsibility for them as well?

I have seen many relationships where the stress for one partner becomes untenable (they get close to resolving their own emotions and learning their own wisdom) while the other partner continue to cruise along with no sense of responsibility. When the partner whose wisdom arrives first, leaves the relationship, the remaining partner is forced to face their own demons and eventually resolve their own emotional issues.

At times facing your own demons means going down a route that is destructive, and it becomes more difficult to turn back, but eventually you have to complete that phase of your own growth. At other times facing your own demons means growing up quickly and getting on with your life.

Either way, you can only take responsibility for the behavior of others up to a point. If you stay in a relationship because you feel obliged to take responsibility for your partner, you stunt the emotional and spiritual growth of your partner.

At this point you need to assess whether it is the right time for YOU to leave the relationship, because your decision, either way, will benefit both you and your partner.

If it is the right time for you to leave, then on a cosmic scale it is also the right time for your partner to remain behind and face their own demons and achieve their own growth.

If it is not the right time for you to leave yet, then it means that you still have unfinished business with your partner. You still have unresolved emotions, prejudices and emotional barriers that you need to break down.

In the long run, neither the decision to stay nor the decision to remain can be right or wrong. What is more important is that you need to understand the reason for remaining in the relationship.

Often traditional relationship counseling focuses on how to keep a relationship going at all costs. If the relationship then fails regardless of all the attempts to the contrary, the focus shifts to survival. Neither of these approaches helps to resolve the emotional issues that need to be resolved when a relationship is ended.

You only move on when you understand what you have gained from the relationship. Only at this point is your soul contract with your partner completed.

 What regrets do you need to let go of?

Fear of the Future

Many people remain in an untenable marriage relationship because they do not know what the future holds. They believe 'rather the devil you know than the devil you don't know'. When they have to justify remaining in a self-destructive relationship, they have many 'yes, but what if . . . '-reasons for not moving on.

Let's look at the process of creating your future. Yes, you do create your future.

When you wake up in the morning, you either get out of bed or you stay in bed. That is the first creative action of your day. From there onwards, everything you do is your creation. You have full control over your mind, body and emotions. You do not even think about most of your actions because they become automated – but you automated them.

At some point you made a decision to do something because it made sense to you or you had some benefit. When the same situation arose, you took the same action, and so a habit was formed – for example brushing your teeth in the morning.

All the decisions you make to create your future have consequences. When you brush your teeth, your breath smells good. When you go to work, you earn money.

Then why do you fear the future when you know it is time to move on?

Because at some time in your life you have added a limiting belief to your decision making process. This limiting belief can take as many shapes as there are people.

We will have a look at the most common limiting beliefs.

  What fears have you had that did not materialize?

I am Unable to Cope By Myself

'I have never paid the bills or mowed the lawn or cooked for myself or taken the car for a service or bought my own clothes. I cannot do that now, because I don't even know where to start.'

Believing that you cannot do something is a very strong belief – as strong as the belief that you can do something. The beliefs are formed in the same way, and the same energy is used to create these beliefs.

How do you undo such beliefs? One step at a time, just like you built them up. Of course a large part of undoing a limiting belief is being willing to risk learning and doing new things.

For example, you might be quite concerned about receiving and having to pay your own bills when you move out of a relationship. You have not paid bills in many years, because that was part of the responsibility your partner took and, and you happily – or reluctantly – relinquished.

However, you would not hesitate to cross a very busy street during peak hours. You will not shy away from providing wisdom and confidence to your children, even if you are not sure yourself.

Or another example: you cannot cook for yourself – you cannot even boil an egg.

However, you are willing to use your judgment to make a decision about a person's life and future during a disciplinary enquiry. You make decisions about how to invest your money and what level of risk to take.

The above examples indicate how we love to create barriers in our own minds. We are the only ones who create those barriers, because we cling to a belief that we

- Do not want to replace

- Do not yet know how to replace

- Do not realize we have replaced already

- Believe makes our lives more comfortable

 What skills will you have to learn (or re-learn) when you leave your relationship?

People Will Avoid Me When I Leave the Relationship

Of course, as a couple you have relationships with various people – family, friends and colleagues.

When you are no longer a couple, people react in different ways.

Here are some of the reactions you can expect:

- Some people will no longer want to associate with you.

  - Your single status reminds them of the flaws in their own relationships. Your courage in breaking free from the relationship forces people to face their own demons, and it is quite easy for them to see you as one of those demons. How they deal with the situation is their choice and not your responsibility. Love them and move on.

  - They may want to finally be honest with you and openly choose sides against you. Do you really need them in your life? Love them and move on.

  - You may find that you have very little in common with them when your partner is out of the picture. Recognize their contribution, love them and move on.

- Some people will want to associate with you because something in the situation resonates with them.

  - They may want more of your time because they revel in pain and they recognize your pain. Initially this is enjoyable because you feel self-righteous – other people think the same way you do, and therefore you must be right. Stay with them for as long as it makes sense to you, but understand that these people are visitors on your path.

- They may want to extend a helping hand because they associate with your experience and want to share their own tricks and tips on coping with the situation. What works for one person does not necessarily work for another person. Listen to these people, but find your own solutions.

- They may want to finally be honest with you and openly choose sides in your favor. Listen to what they have to say, and do not become judgmental. Rather use them to learn more about yourself.

- They may recognize the new you and want to associate with you to reinforce your own healing. Open yourself up to the experience and allow your intuition to recognized people who resonate with the true you.

Married people or people in a long-term relationship often stay in a painful relationship because they are concerned about the reaction of their family and friends when they leave the relationship.

Let's look at this from a different point of view – of course!

John and Anne have been married for twenty years. John's job takes him away from home during the week, leaving Anne to deal with the household and their three children. Over weekends John mows the lawn, watches sports and rests – because he works so hard during the week.

They have not had sex in three years. They hardly even talk to each other when they are together during weekends. When they do talk, it escalates in a shouting match.

Each of the teenage children reacts to the situation in their own way, and Anne has her hands full with them.

You can add from your own experience here.

Anne has suggested marriage counseling but John refused. She has read a number of those self-help books and tried the sexy underwear, the surprise gifts and so on and so on – all turned out to be damp squibs. She is ready to call it quits.

Anne has told her mother, Mary, about the situation, but Mary reminded Anne of her wedding vows – together 'until death us do part'. Anne knows that her parents' marriage has been troubled for years. She has seen how Mary has aged from the strain of holding it all together and she does not want to follow the same route.

Now take a step back and look at the situation again. Mary has bought into the fantasy that a marriage must last as long as both people are alive. Mary refuses to change her thinking, because she is concerned about her friends abandoning her. Mary's friends share the same beliefs and troubles.

If Anne decides to leave John, she might just have the audacity to explain why she does that, and she might even have the courage to create a new, less stressed life for herself and her children. What would that do to Mary's value system? It would expose Mary's life as a farce, and her marriage as a nightmare rather than a happy fantasy. Mary would have to re-think her own marriage.

On the other hand, if Anne does what a 'good' wife does and stays with John, then there is no need for anyone to ask too many uncomfortable questions. Everyone can continue to strive towards their unrealistic fantasy, no matter how painful it is.

In a quantum process, we stay in a state of maximum stress when we refuse to let go of blockages that inhibit the flow of energy. We will not resolve an emotion and reach that moment of gratitude and enlightenment as long as we hold on to the blockages.

What happens when our energy does not flow freely in and around our bodies?

Imagine a group of children forming a circle and tossing a ball around the circle. Each child expectantly holds their hands out to catch the ball. However, little Elmo is having a worse than usual day and he refuses to even put his hands out.

The other children believe that if they keep tossing the ball to him, Elmo will join in the fun and catch the ball.

Johnny passes the ball on to Elmo, who refuses to catch it. The ball bounces back to Johnny, who passes the ball to Elmo again, this time a bit harder. This continues for a while, with Johnny throwing the ball harder each time, and eventually hurting Elmo, who still refuses to play along.

Then the children decide to try the other way round. They pass the ball anti-clockwise, and this time Jenny passes the ball to Elmo. However, Elmo still refuses to play along, and no matter how loud the children shout or how hard Jenny throws the ball, Elmo sticks to his position, even though it hurts him every time the ball comes his way.

Eventually the game disintegrates and everyone blames Elmo for this. Nobody asks Elmo why he refuses to catch the ball, and he believes nobody will listen to his reason for refusing to play along.

What could Elmo's reasons be?

Imagine that each of the children in the circle represents a part of your body, and the movement around the circle (both clockwise and anti-clockwise) represents the flow of energy around your body.

Does Elmo represent

- Your regular headaches, migraine, sinusitis, even a brain tumour (because your circumstances are 'doing your head in'?

- Your regular laryngitis or chest infection (because you feel 'smothered'?)

- Your angina or irregular heartbeat or heart cramps (because the situation is 'heart-breaking'?

- Your constipation, indigestion or food allergies (because you 'cannot stomach' any more of the situation?)

- Your kidney stones, water retention or lower back ache, (because you are constantly 'pissed off'?)

- Your weak back, back ache or osteoporosis (because you are 'not getting any support'?)

- Your arthritis, Parkinson's disease or sciatica (because the situation is 'crippling you'?)

And you can add to the list and ask your own questions. See how beautifully our language expresses our emotional and energy blockages?

If you want to stay in a relationship well past its well-by date, you should expect your own little Elmo to stop 'playing the game'. Which is the bigger price you pay – accepting that each relationship has its own shelf-life, no matter what people say, or living with the tension of a 'failed' relationship and paying the medical bills?

The decision to stay or leave is yours and yours only, no matter what 'the people' say.

What physical expression do you give to your energy blockage? Where in your body is the blockage? What does this blockage tell you about yourself?

I Do Not Have Enough Money

Many people stay in a relationship far too long because they firmly believe that they cannot afford financially to move on.

But let us take a step back. Remember when you were a young adult and you left home or finished studying? You believed that you would get a job so that you would earn an income and take care of yourself. And you did.

There were times when the money was tight. What did you do? You managed. You worked harder and earned more. You scaled down on luxuries and economized. You borrowed money and paid back the loans. You found bargains. You took care of yourself, and later of your children as well. You had to. You were resourceful.

You asked for help, and later on when you were in a position to do so, you helped others.

Now you cling to a relationship or marriage that has come to a natural end, because you convinced yourself that if you leave, you will not survive financially.

If this objection is repeated for long enough it becomes a self-fulfilling prophecy.

On the other hand, if you start to recall different ways in which you have managed and coped over the years, you will find that you always have the required resources. Chances are good that the mental block related to money is only attached to your relationship, and that in all other areas of your life you manage financially.

Is your marriage one of those that are held together by legislation which makes it too expensive to get a divorce? How do you define 'too expensive'?

What is really keeping you in the relationship when you recognize that even though at times money was tight, you did manage? Think about it and deal with that reason rather than with the excuse that you 'cannot afford financially' to let go of your relationship.

Could it be that the **financial gain** ⋂ from staying in the relationship overshadows the **emotional loss** ⋃? If that is the case, you will find an **emotional gain** ⋂ and a **financial loss** ⋃ in the same situation, because there is always balance.

 How can you earn more money? Don't give up on this one before you have even started!

I Cannot Be Alone

When your relationship comes to a natural end, you are not left on your own. You still have relationships with other people, for example friends, colleagues or relatives. However, every relationship you have has a specific purpose.

The end of your relationship means that you are faced with recognizing the purpose of that relationship. If you still have unresolved issues related to the person or the situation, those issues become larger than life and you are forced to deal with them.

We often hold on to a relationship because we are afraid of dealing with those issues. We do not want to be alone because we fear the thoughts that we have been suppressing for a long time. We fear the fact that we need to redefine our lives. We do not acknowledge our own power and the fact that we plan and create our lives every day.

When you leave a relationship and a person behind, you have a few options.

The first option is to get used to your own company and confront the self-talk and programming about yourself.

While you are in a relationship, there is a rhythm to the interaction between you and the other person. You know what to expect, and you know how to act – like in a well-practiced dance routine.

When the relationship ends, the music stops. You only have yourself to dance with. You can resist this and make yourself very unhappy, or you can open yourself up to new experiences and learn to dance by yourself.

Suddenly having your own company after ending a relationship can be a painful, exhausting experience when you see yourself as a victim. It does not come as a surprise that widowed or divorced people often develop health issues after the separation from their spouses.

Their attitude is often that they are dealing with the end of a relationship and on top of that they are also physically unwell. The truth is that they are physically unwell because of the way they deal with the end of the relationship.

You need to accept that the end of a relationship can have a physical impact on your body. The way to deal with that is to be aware of exactly where the discomfort is, and to use that information to find the cause of the discomfort.

Of course the other option is to see your new single status as a gift and discover the true you. For some people this is a scary thought, because they have no idea what they will discover.

Some relationships are quite demanding and the only way you can deal with it is to compromise. Over time you lose your identity and individuality, and you forget who you are. When you are suddenly single again, it is like meeting a stranger in the mirror. All the things that you compromised on now need to be faced and redefined.

Now that you are aware of the process of resolving emotions and how emotional cycles are completed, you will also know that when a spiral is resolved, you achieve a higher vibration and you meet more of your true self.

How does your true self look? In this respect we are all the same – our true self is pure, unconditional Love.

For us to achieve this state of unconditional Love, we need to rid ourselves of all barriers, preconceived ideas, emotional obstacles and prejudices.

That is the most challenging part of being single again. Every time you look in the mirror, you become aware of another aspect that you need to resolve. If you are brave enough to face that duality or division inside of yourself, you move another step closer to integration. If you choose to rather live with the duality, you tend to find other people who support that same duality, and the duality continues. But you pay a physical, emotional and spiritual price for staying in that situation.

There is a second option. You can go straight into another relationship and be disillusioned if it turns out to be the same as the previous one.

If you have not resolved a specific inner conflict yet, you will continue to have the same or a similar situation over and over again until you have gained your wisdom.

For example, you have a relationship with a person who is violent. Of course the situation did not start out like this. Your partner was initially quite loving and caring. Then there was a stressful situation and your partner became violent because they had no other way of dealing with the stress. You got the fright of your life, and wanted to leave, but they apologized and things went back to normal – until the next incident happened. With each incident the level of violence against you escalated until there was a crisis and you left the relationship.

You did not take any time to reflect on the situation, and of course all the blame was to be laid on a violent person who could not cope with stress.

Then you had another relationship – this time with verbal violence, but the pattern was the same – peace, then stress, then verbal violence that escalated and so on.

And this pattern could continue for a very long time.

But take a step back. Of course the lesson may be different for each person in such a situation and this is one example.

At some level you allowed this person to deny your self-worth, because you never felt comfortable with expressing the fact that you are a strong, resourceful, wise creature of God. However, after having had these experiences, you one day realize that God did not make a mistake when you were created. You feel that incredibly good surge of inner strength, and you just know 'in your bones' that you deserve the best.

And then you meet a person who affirms this inner strength all the time. You expect nothing else, because you know who you are. The pattern is broken.

Where you have had a series of similar relationships, it is time to sit back and figure out how those relationships have changed you for the better. What have you learned about yourself from those relationships? Once you have gained the wisdom, you may or may not have another relationship. If you do have another relationship, the pattern will be broken. If you don't have another relationship, you will have a much clearer sense of your own identity, and you will be happy with the person you are.

Taking all your baggage into a new relationship is also unfair to your new partner.

Rather take time out to become familiar with who you really are. Do things that will show Love to your inner child. Identify all the things that you are afraid of and do them – break that fear. This may not be easy initially, but as you succeed you will gather courage and try your hand at more and more things that you did not think you could do.

What do you enjoy doing on your own?

When I Leave My Partner May Self-Harm

Many people stay in a relationship because they are afraid that their partner will actually go through with their threat to self-harm.

When these threats cloud the issues, they become emotional blackmail. Of course some people will in fact go through with their threats and self-harm. Whether you stay in a relationship or leave the relationship and leave the person behind, they will self-harm, because that is how they choose to get attention focused on them.

You already know that when confronted with a situation, you always have a choice of reactions. Exactly the same applies to your partner. They also choose how to react to your leaving.

You already know what staying in the relationship is doing to you. Staying in the relationship and not breaking free is a choice, just as leaving the relationship is a choice. The same applies to your partner.

You already know that at times protecting a person against harm does more harm than exposing them to the situation, because being exposed to the situation results in their emotional and spiritual growth. Yes, we do need to care for other people, but when you know that your continued caring is becoming destructive, who gains from the situation? Nobody.

 Do you in some way take responsibility for your partner's behavior?

We Need to Stay Together For the Sake of the Children

Couples who stay together for the sake of the children do not fool their children or anybody else. They only fool themselves, because those couples hold on to a fantasy that has outlived its shelf life.

Living in a fantasy world requires a huge amount of energy, because the real world does not go away. You need to maintain the fantasy of a happy, united marriage for the world to see, as well as the daily reality of a tense, divided situation behind closed doors.

Where there are children from a relationship, those children also have a soul contract with their parents. The children came into this world with their own agendas and their own choice of wisdom to experience. Where parents are obviously unhappy in a marriage, the children are very aware of the situation. Of course the children will grow and gain their own wisdom from the situation, but often the actions (or inertia) of the unhappy parents delay the growth of the entire family unit.

 How will you and your children gain from the end of your relationship?

What Did You Gain From the Relationship?

Your major gain from your relationship is when you better understand who you are.

When a relationship breaks up, the easiest way out is to blame the other person for not living up to your expectations. However, there are always two people in a relationship. You will truly have gained when you recognize your own role in the relationship and discern what the purpose of the relationship was for you.

Judging the other person assumes that they have done something wrong, when in fact everything is perfectly designed to teach us what we are meant to learn.

Judging yourself assumes that you are guilty of something or have done something wrong, when in fact the purpose of the relationship was to highlight an inner conflict that needed to be resolved. There is nothing wrong with having such an inner conflict – it would be like saying that crawling is wrong and walking is right, when in fact crawling precedes walking.

The question is: what have you learned from the relationship? How did the interaction with this person help you to become who you are?

Staying in a relationship at all costs stunts your own growth. It also stunts the growth of your partner, because you both stay in a state of limbo, hoping that your reality will change into the fantasy that you are not having.

The end of a relationship forces you to find your own inner resources and trust yourself.

When a relationship ends and you are able to resolve all residual emotions, you are ready to either start a next relationship, or be happy with not being in a specific relationship with a person. Until you have reached this stage of gratitude and bliss, you are still in a relationship, even if you think you have put it behind you.

You are also still in a relationship if you allow that cord which binds you to your partner to remain in place.

You will repeat the same sort of relationship with different people until you have recognized the wisdom that you needed to integrate in yourself.

Part of the wisdom you discover in yourself is that it is OK to ask for and accept help on any aspect of your life.

Do you need advice on your finances? It is OK to ask other people in similar situations how they are coping.

Do you need help with stress management? How about asking a friend for a massage? Have you thought on reading up about food that are nutritious and affordable? While you work on finding your balance again, your body changes and your stress levels go up and down. Have you always taken your body for granted? Maybe now is the time to become more aware of your body as not who you are, but rather as the container of who you are. Do you really want to store the precious gemstone of your spirit in a rusty jam tin of a body?

When did you last do something to spoil yourself? This does not need to involve any additional expenses. It could be something as simple as a bubble bath or walking in a garden or going to the cinema on your own.

Are you using this time of change as an opportunity to discover who you really are? Have you ever tried meditation or yoga? Do you keep a diary, so that you can write down your dreams and insights and discoveries?

The end of a relationship is the ideal time to become truly self-indulgent. Of course you can spend your time feeling quite guilty about this, or you can remind yourself that if you pour new wine in a used container, the wine will turn sour.

Use the opportunity to clear out all the baggage you are carrying, so that you can fill up with everything that you have missed and everything that you want to explore. That is one of the great blessings of no longer being in a relationship. It is also an opportunity to thank your partner for now having the space to explore who you have become as a result of the relationship.

It does take a while to find your balance again after you have ended a relationship. Of course, if you are wise, you will spend the time finding the missing side of the coin, in other words identifying the hidden sides of the experiences from the relationship that stand out for you.

During this period of recovery you will accept and respect your choices. You will also gain insight into and respect the other person's choices. You will discover the true meaning of Love.

You will discover that the greatest Love of all is indeed learning to Love yourself.

Chapter 7: The Future of Relationships

In this chapter you will learn:

- How the nature of relationships is changing

- How the Law of Change works

- Why we need to focus on the purpose of a relationship rather than use the relationship as a crutch

Have you recently said to someone 'Where has the time gone?'? Have you noticed how the period between one Christmas and the next seems to be shrinking?

Time is being compressed. Time is moving faster. This has to do with changes in the magnetic field of the earth, which is the result of the movement of the planets.

These changes result in everything happening faster than we have ever experienced. Technology is impacting on everything, including our relationships.

For example, an estimated one in eight couples who marry in the US has met online. There were 65.8 million marriages in the United States in 2009. This means 8.225 million couples met on the internet.

Married couples who met online have an average courtship period of 18.5 months. For married couples who met offline their courtship period last on average 42 months. These couples also were most probably on their second marriage.

And that does not mean everyone in the US has internet access – in fact, in December 2009 the US was only ranked number 19 in the world in terms of internet access to citizens.

In the UK there were 8 million single people in 2008. They went on 24 million first dates with 69% being arranged through online dating and social networks.

Roughly 40 million American single people use online dating and social networking sites to meet new people.

More text messages are being sent per DAY than there are people on the planet. Relationships are formed and ended around some of these messages.

People more often encounter situations where they need to form short-term relationships.

For example, one in four employees has been with their current employers for less than a year. It is estimated that the young people of today will have had an estimated ten to 14 jobs by the age of 38. This indicates short-term relationships in the work place.

Where people share the same experience due to e.g. a natural disaster such as a tsunami, flood, earthquake, or the volcanic ash that stopped air travel recently, short-term, highly focused relationships are formed.

 Have you recently had to form a short but intense relationship with someone as a result of some crisis? What did you discover about yourself?

If you have not had the above experience yet, you are aware of how natural disasters impact on people's lives. While looking at these disasters from a distance, what went through your mind? What emotions did you experience? How could you relate to the people involved? How did the awareness of these events shape your view of yourself?

We no longer have time to use relationships as crutches to cover our insecurities and weaknesses. We have to look at relationships as a means of growing rapidly towards discovering who we are.

We can no longer jump to conclusions about the other party and in so doing get rid of our responsibilities in a relationship. We need to focus on our own agendas and discover our own wisdom from the relationship.

Quantum changes as a result of relationships are happening faster than ever. Being aware of these changes help us get the best out of a relationship while we are in it, and also when we end the relationship.

Changes in how we experience and view relationships result in purer, less cluttered relationships. Each relationship has a very specific purpose, and the quickest way to recover from a relationship is to identify that purpose and accept the natural life cycle of the relationship.

If we continue to look at 'new' relationships with 'old' eyes, we will continue to see only failure. A relationship can only 'fail' if we make no effort to understand the purpose of the relationship. In this sense it is not the relationship that fails, but rather the perception of the people in the relationship that is flawed.

We need to be much more aware of the physical dis-ease in our bodies that result from the way we deal with our relationships.

These physical symptoms give us clues on which aspect of the relationship we need to focus on to resolve an inner conflict and move on. Rather than grab some prescription medication, go inside and discover what wisdom you need to gain. Once you understand the lesson, the symptoms will dissolve and you will have more energy to focus on your life purpose.

 What is your body telling you about your relationship? Where do you need to focus and gain your wisdom?

Where there is a difference between our inner world and the world around us, we experience stress. That stress can only be resolved by getting our inner and outer worlds aligned. We are very seldom in a position where the outer world changes to suit us. We are always in a position where we can eliminate a perceived obstacle or boundary and remove the stress. That is the purpose of a relationship. This is also one of the laws of karma, or spiritual laws, which states: *to grow, you must change – not the people, things or environment around you.*

In this sense, a relationship is meant to sharpen our senses. More and more often we will be using our relationships to identify our own inner tensions, and then we use our senses to gather more information to resolve that tension. If we are not aware of the process, we may be using those same senses to gather information that will increase the tension.

 What perception, rule or prejudice do you feel you need to change as a result of your relationship?

Because time is moving faster, the natural life cycle of all relationships is also moving faster. As a result our relationship experiences are becoming far more intense. Some relationships are with us for life, but most relationships will only be part of our memory for life. If those memories are shrouded in emotions and imbalanced, our lives will also become more and more imbalanced.

Knowledge of how relationships work and why we have them will remove much insecurity about the future. Of course we will still have feelings of insecurity about the future, but we will have a choice. Do we approach the future with fear and trepidation, or with excitement? We use the same energy for both. We are in a position to choose. We do not have much time to choose, because time is shrinking.

In conclusion: if you stay in your relationship, may it be for reasons that resonate with you and bring you much inner peace. If you leave your relationship behind, it will be because you have grasped your own inner wisdom and you are ready to move on. Either way, you are fully responsible for your future. Make the best of it for yourself.

Blessings to you.

About The Author

Elsabe Smit is a well-known international coach, facilitator, author, and public speaker that uses her clairvoyant and intuitive skills in her daily life to assist all of those that she comes into contact with in her professional life.

She has an MBA (Master Business Administration), a MA in Industrial Psychology, and extensive experience as a Business Analyst. Using all her knowledge, skills and competencies, Elsabe helps people to understand the mysteries of life and Love, so that they can regain control of their lives.

Elsabe Smit was born and raised in South Africa, but has since 2000 been living in the UK.

After years of facing numerous personal challenges, involving her relationship with her drug- and alcohol-addicted mother, living with and getting divorced from an abusive husband, being a single mother, being a mistress for a period of time, and then facing unemployment, she one day realised that she had been given the amazing gift of intuition and clairvoyance.

Using her newly discovered gifts, she then rediscovered herself. She learned that all her past experiences, "good" and "bad", were only stepping stones on her life's blueprint towards loving and accepting herself.

Having always having had a keen interest in human behaviour, this discovery took her on a different path, adding the study of life, death and spirituality to her interests. During that journey she explored NLP and embraced Quantum Physics. Elsabe studied some of the world's best acknowledged researchers and gurus in the fields of relationships, health and business.

During her professional life Elsabe's career included lecturing at a South African University, being a Human Resources Manager with a mining house and a multinational security firm, and being a freelance business analyst.

In between the various permanent positions and contracts, she developed her reputation as a sought after author, speaker, facilitator, coach and mentor.

As an author, some of her books are today still in use as prescribed text books for university and college students in South Africa. Other books have been published and are available on Amazon, and some books have been published as E-books which she shares as free gifts.

As a speaker, facilitator and trainer she has presented numerous programmes to groups ranging from a dozen to hundreds of people. The subject matter has been as varied and interesting as her life.

As a mentor, she coached and mentored small business owners, blue-chip executives and employees covering a myriad of professions, employment levels and industries.

Don't forget her contribution to the world of **psychics**. She's been on various radio and TV shows with international audiences. In addition, Elsabe has done thousands of personal psychic readings for people from all walks of life located in more than 80 countries - including one for a death row inmate in a US prison.

Throughout her life Elsabe has been passionately focused on identifying the nuances that make a difference in people lives, the why's of birth, life and death - and now it's your turn to tap into the vast wealth of knowledge and experiences that she has gained during her lifetime, so that like Elsabe ...

YOU can also **Discover yourself and Love YOUR Life**.

If you have questions, or comments, contact Elsabe at elsabe@elsabesmit.com, or visit her website at www.elsabesmit.com to access her skill so that you can resolve your burning issue.

You can also follow Elsabe on Twitter or LinkedIn or YouTube or Google+

More from This Author

If you would like to experience the practical application of Elsabe's wisdom, get yourself a copy of the book *Resilience: How to Restore and Keep Your Faith in Yourself and Your Business Idea*. It's available on the Kindle Store now.

Self-Employed? Ever felt frustrated, isolated - even desperate on occasion with no-one to turn to for help, guidance or support? If so, then this powerful, practical book will help you to keep moving forwards and living your dream.

Ask yourself the following questions:

- How do you take your business from brain to heart to stellar?

- Where does forgiveness feature in your business plan?

- Why do bad things happen to good people, despite their best intentions?

- What if the business idea you have put your heart and soul into goes wrong?

- Who do you turn to for advice and how can you keep on track in the face of adversity?

The powerful, proven, practical and highly effective concepts, techniques, and spiritual principles in this book can be applied to almost every commercial problem, issue or challenge that you will face in starting and running your own business.

Real world, practical examples and exercises are included for you to personalize and apply to your current circumstances.

Ever been anxious, frustrated or worried about:

- What makes you really "different" or unique in your marketplace?

- Deciding and accepting what you really offer potential customers?

- Finding, winning and keeping Customers?

- Charging (and getting paid) what you're really worth?

- Juggling home life with running a business?

- Making the right decision at the right time?

- Getting paid for work already done?

- Personal and professional conflict?

- Allowing your fears to prevent you from achieving your goals?

- Dealing with the emotional stress of starting and running your own business?

- Learning to know, like and trust yourself?

"Resilience: How To Restore And Keep Faith In Yourself & Your Business Idea" shares a common sense approach that simply isn't common practice among the millions of self-employed facing the daily issues, challenges & obstacles of self-employment that are holding them back and preventing them from achieving their personal, professional and commercial goals and objectives.

Discover:

- How to make sense of conflict - since you cannot avoid it

- How to turn rejection into opportunity

- When do you celebrate success and when to navigate hurdles for even greater success

- Where to find inspired answers and solutions

- How you can prepare for meetings knowing the outcome in advance

- When to walk away and when to fight back, and why

- What the real "lessons" are that you need to master, to guarantee your personal success

- How to reassure yourself, your family or your loved ones that you're mentally prepared for the challenges presented to you, your finances or your health

You want to work for yourself and you want to be in control of your own destiny.

We know it, you know it & your heart knows it!

Do you want to live the life and lifestyle you've always craved?

You've already got the power & resilience to succeed in self-employment.

You just need to recognize it, and be shown how to use it.

In the UK: Use this link to buy:
http://www.amazon.co.uk/Resilience-restore-faith-yourself-business-ebook/dp/B00J98FZ3G/

Outside the UK: Use this link to buy:
http://www.amazon.com/Resilience-restore-faith-yourself-business-ebook/dp/B00J98FZ3G/

www.ingramcontent.com/pod-product-compliance
Lightning Source LLC
Chambersburg PA
CBHW070431290526
45791CB00005B/1919